SHAKESPEARE
TO TEACH OR NOT TO TEACH

TEACHING SHAKESPEARE MADE FUN

From Elementary to High School

— NEWLY REVISED —

CASS FOSTER & LYNN G. JOHNSON

We would like to thank the following individuals for their kind cooperation in helping us understand what works best in introducing Shakespeare to children:

Pamela Bowen, Amy Bryan, Janet Campbell, Cassandra Casto, Louise Conti (Principal), Sheri Edwards, Janet Eitelgeorge, Robert Kelly (principal), Professor Rick Koehler, Mary Anne Luce, Monica Ludwick, Julie McCready, Professor Andrew McLean, Sharon Mollica, Stephanie Morris, Kathy Pryor, Lynn Riggenbauch (principal), Sandy Weaver, Rick Wair (principal) and Deborah Wilhelm.

First edition, 1992.
Second edition, 1994.

All rights reserved. Printed in the United States of America.

Library of Congress Cataloging-in-Publication Data

Foster, Cass, 1948 -
     Shakespeare—to teach or not to teach: grades 3 and up / Cass Foster and Lynn G. Johnson. — 1st ed. p. cm. "Designed to supplement the Shakespeare for children series"
Note to teachers.
     Includes bibliographical references (p. 119).
     ISBN 1-877749-03-6 : $19.95
     1. Shakespeare, William. 1564-1616 — Study and teaching (Elementary) — Outlines, syllabi, etc. 2. Activity programs in education. 3. Drama in education. I. Johnson, Lynn G. 1947-
II. Title.
PR2987.F67 1992
372.64'044—dc20   91-30940
                                                              CIP

Photographs reproduced with permission of
The Folger Shakespeare Library

Five Star Publications, 4696 W. Tyson Street, Chandler, AZ 85226
(602) 940-8182.

Edited by Mary E. Hawkins
Cover Illustration by Robert Doe
Typesetting by Two Macs Type & Design

About the Authors

Cass Foster, author of the **Shakespeare for Children** series, is the head of the Theatre Department at a small liberal arts college in central Arizona. Besides serving as an adjunct faculty member in the theatre department at Arizona State University, he is actively involved in the theatre community as a director and fight choreographer. Cass earned a Bachelor's degree in Drama from the University of Washington and a Master of Fine Arts in Directing from the University of Illinois, Champaign-Urbana.

Lynn G. Johnson is an Associate Professor of Early and Middle Childhood Education at The Ohio State University at Mansfield. He teaches a variety of Child Development, Early Childhood Education and Elementary Education courses. Currently his research focuses on creative children and early childhood special education. Lynn earned his Bachelors and Masters degrees in Elementary Education from Wilkes College, a Masters degree in Elementary Counseling from Marywood College, and a Ph.D. in Early Childhood Education and Child Development from Indiana State University.

These methodologies work with teachers that have had absolutely no experience with Shakespeare. Nearly every teacher we have observed began with a great deal of anxiety and doubt. In most cases both those elements were eliminated after the first session with **Shakespeare for Children**.

We recommend introducing this material as early as the fourth grade. However, we have observed successful applications as early as the second grade. Obviously much depends on the students' background, the instructor's interests, and the administration's attitude towards whole-language based curriculums.

Dedicated

Note to Teachers

This text has been designed to supplement the SHAKESPEARE FOR CHILDREN series (C. Foster, Five Star Publications, Chandler, Arizona, 1989) but these methodologies can be used in conjunction with any situation involving the introduction of Shakespeare from elementary education up to, and including, the high school level.

The methods here are also effective in situations where more than one grade level at the same school wants to work with the SHAKESPEARE FOR CHILDREN series. When fourth and fifth grade teachers are concerned about third graders coming to them having already studied the play, we have a simple solution. Each grade level might incorporate activities from a different area in the curriculum, i.e., the third graders would explore art-related activities, while the fourth graders explore creative-writing and the fifth graders supplement their studies with social studies-type activities. Do keep in mind, as the children grow, they will gain new insights, appreciation and skills each time they study the play.

Table of Contents

Teacher's Notes

Value of Shakespeare

Shakespeare presented his plays to everyone: The educated, illiterate, wealthy, poor, young and old. It seems audiences these days are dwindling. Today's college professors grow more and more weary over the amount of spoonfeeding involved in presenting Shakespeare to students. High school administrators often find themselves struggling with anxiety-stricken teachers that don't feel competent to teach Shakespeare, while numerous elementary and secondary teachers are grateful they aren't expected to work with material that seems best suited for Ph.D.s.

Fortunately there are numerous exceptions to the rule. When we began to explore what was being done with Shakespeare prior to the college level, we discovered some highly innovative and inspiring individuals working with Shakespeare as early as third grade. They wanted to turn children on to good literature. They were doing remarkable work introducing children to the intriguing plots of Shakespeare as well as to his fascinating characters and relevant themes.

These educators are real pioneers in our educational system. What these rare individuals still weren't doing, for the most part, was introducing Shakespeare with Shakespeare's own language. Their reasons are certainly legitimate. They either didn't understand the language, weren't convinced the children would understand the language, or did not think the original language was necessary.

This leaves the teacher interested in whole-language based material and Shakespeare with two choices: Introduce Shakespeare with the language contemporized or do not introduce Shakespeare. **Shakespeare for Children** presents a third choice: Using Shakespeare's own language while condensing the plays.

Many people believe that Shakespeare's writing may not be appropriate for children; however, our experience and the experiences related to us by teachers who make Shakespeare a part of their curriculum suggest otherwise. The only limitations that experts place on literature for children is that it reflect the emotions and experiences of today's youth. Children must be able to understand and relate their experiences to the content of the story. Current children's literature reflects the problems of today's world and its children: Problems that children read about in newspapers and magazines, see on television, movies, and videos, and experience at home and in school (Huck, Helpler and Hickman, 1987).

Shakespeare addressed numerous problems of his day; problems related to love, death, parental conflict, rebellion against authority, and power. These concerns are universal in nature and not confined to a specific century or era. They are also concerns experienced by children. An author with the gift to portray these experiences "with imagination and insight, give them literary shape and structure, and communicate them to children is writing children's literature" (Huck, et al. 1987, p. 6).

Children are naturally curious about such aspects of life. What we offer is a healthy, non-threatening manner to explore these issues.

Although Shakespeare didn't expressly write for children, the **Shakespeare for Children** series selects exciting and interesting action, condenses the content, adds related illustrations, and offers supplementary activities that enhance children's interest in and understanding of Shakespeare's works. Selected Shakespearean works condensed by the first author also meet other important characteristics of children's literature.

A major concern in our early attempts to introduce Shakespeare to children was how they would respond to the difficult vocabulary. We feared that children, or for that matter teachers, might feel stymied by words they couldn't pronounce or understand. A glossary of terms helped alleviate this concern, but also, children seemed to enjoy the challenge of "different" words if the teacher modeled an interest and enthusiasm for such words. As E.B. White contends:

Some writers for children deliberately avoid using words they think a child doesn't know. This emasculates the prose and... bores the reader... Children love words that give them a hard time, provided they are in a context that absorbs their attention (Haviland, 1973, p. 140).

So, absorbing context is a key to unlocking the meaning of new or difficult words. We have noticed that children become absorbed with the SHAKESPEARE FOR CHILDREN series if the teacher brings the story to life with supplemental activities (to be discussed later in this manual) and an enthusiastic presentation. Shakespeare's classic works are good literature. Such literature has both educational and personal value for children.

Research points to the educational value of literature in aiding the development of children's language, reading, and writing. Children who are frequently exposed to high quality literature tend to develop high linguistic competence. This exposure can be either first-hand or can involve being read to. Likewise, the more experience a child has with literature, the more the child will be able to comprehend story meaning and predict upcoming story events. Children also tend to increase creative writing ability while reading, hearing, and discussing quality literature (Mills, 1974). The development of composition writing requires reading and/or being read to. Children use the written language of others as models for their own writing (Smith, 1982).

Although literature has proven educational value, it also enriches the personal lives of children. For one thing, literature makes children's lives more enjoyable. It takes them places they can't visit or haven't been yet. It opens up new horizons for children, making their education an entertaining endeavor. By turning children on to literature, we can initiate a behavior that lends to a lifetime of pleasure (Huck, et al., 1987).

Literature also helps develop children's creative imagination. It motivates them to consider people and events in new and different ways. Literature, unlike television which leaves very little to children's imaginations, allows and encourages children to paint their own mental landscapes of story content (Huck, et al., 1987). Children are free to imagine, not constrained by a set image prescribed for them.

Literature provides vicarious experiences for children which give them new perspectives on life. Literature can transport children to a different place and time from where they normally reside. Children are free to travel roads filled with mystery, adventure, excitement, sadness, glory or humor in the safety of their own room, but they return feeling different, more complete and experienced. They will have gained an increased awareness of how others live, a greater sense of compassion, and therefore, a better understanding of themselves. Their whole being will be affected. As Huck, Helpler, and Hickman (1987, p. 9) suggest, "Literature is concerned with feeling, the quality of life. It can educate the heart as well as the mind." Shakespeare has educated the heart and mind of adults for over four centuries. He can do the same thing for children.

As stated before, we like to keep Shakespeare and the flavor of his language intact as much as possible. This can't happen if Shakespeare is introduced by contemporizing the language. So let us briefly explore the results of contemporizing Shakespeare.

First of all, contemporizing the language reinforces the notion the verse is beyond the students' comprehension; that they aren't expected to understand the language or that the language is intended for a specially trained group of interested students. Quite simply, they perceive Shakespeare's writings as a foreign language. How many of us are willing or would even contemplate studying a foreign language in order to comprehend or appreciate a few plays?

Changing the language suggests, either explicitly or implicitly, that the verse is not a vital ingredient in Shakespeare's plays. It overlooks the fact that his language was carefully constructed to contain a rhythm, a musical quality (if you will), that on both a conscious and subconscious level, carries us through the brilliance and depths of his writings. Mood, pace, characterization, and interpretation are directly connected to the language - as it was written.

Finally, language change denies children the opportunity to explore the beauty and genius of Shakespeare's verse before they learn they are not supposed to be able to understand his plays. Shakespeare, for goodness sake, was a poet. While his story-lines are certainly important, he was a master with a pen. His words and the combination of those words contain a treasure that just can't be found elsewhere. Shakespeare was the greatest playwright to ever live. Let us respect him and his works by sharing as much of him as we can, rather than as little of him as we can.

The language in the **Shakespeare for Children** series is condensed but not altered. Narration is used to help interpret the action, and illustrations are employed to help the reader visualize the story. Eventually you will want to encourage the students to read and explore the full-length versions.

Before moving into recommended methodologies, we would like to proceed with some background information on the Middle Ages, English Renaissance, Elizabethan England, and, of course, Shakespeare himself.

Middle Ages

The Middle Ages generally mean the years between A.D. 500 and 1500. During this period there was very little in the way of theatre. In fact there was very little in the way of culture. The first half of the Middle Ages, known as the Dark Ages, was a lawless and foreboding time.

Schools, churches, civic buildings and theatres were all destroyed by the Barbarians. Education was left to monks; religion was fairly confined to monasteries hidden in forests; and acting was usually restricted to singers and dancers that would travel from town to town. There was little law and order. The only real law was survival of the fittest.

People, for the most part, were not well educated and not terribly conscious of hygiene. Plagues would come and go, wiping out large segments of the population. The average life expectancy for the lower classes was thirty years. The upper classes could expect to live to an average of thirty-five years. Under these conditions it made perfect sense to marry and have children at an early age.

It was in the last half of the Middle Ages that the church started to get back on its feet and regain wealth and power. Since few could read or understand Latin, the church used performers to act out Biblical stories. These productions, that would often be performed on the streets as pageants, would not only teach the Bible, they would teach lessons in morality.

English Renaissance
(1485-1649)

The English Renaissance brought the Middle Ages to a close. Instead of looking to religion for the answers to life, society was starting to explore itself and the world around it. Men and women were looking within, trying to understand who they were so they could recognize and realize their full potential, though perhaps they didn't use those words.

The Renaissance was marked by invention and exploration; renewed interest in art, in theatre and in the potential of humankind. Much time and thought went into duplicating the classical rules of ancient Greek theatre.

The Greeks would not combine comedy with tragedy, they would not permit violence on the stage, and there could only be one plot to the story. The neoclassic rules were strictly adhered to in Spain and Italy but France and England were a different story.

Shakespeare and his contemporaries not only combined comedy with their tragedies, they would stage magnificent fight scenes. Shakespeare's plays also contain numerous plots, though they are all connected and resolved by the play's end. Shakespeare was a master at entertaining his audiences.

Elizabethan England

The Elizabethan era is named after the ruling monarch, Queen Elizabeth I, who ruled from 1558 to 1603. During the time of Shakespeare there was a great deal of unrest in England centered around recognition of England's official religion. In order to control the civil unrest Queen Elizabeth declared that no plays could contain material that dealt with contemporary religious or political figures.

It was common for plays that dealt with one particular religion to arouse the audience to riot in the streets. This created a problem for contemporary playwrights, since very few plays were of a secular (non-religious) nature.

The Elizabethan theatre was quite successful until 1642, when the Puritans, led by Oliver Cromwell, removed Charles I from the throne and closed down all theatres. It was their belief that if the theatre failed to remind people of G-d, then the theatre was of the devil.

Cromwell and his Puritan followers controlled England from 1642 to 1660. In 1649 they beheaded Charles I, but in 1660 Charles II was allowed to take over the throne. The eighteen years England had no monarch is known as the Interregnum. Charles II's ascension to the throne (the restoring of the monarchy) marked the start of the Restoration Period.

Ex dono Willi Jaggard Typographi: aᵒ 1623

Mr. WILLIAM
SHAKESPEARES
COMEDIES,
HISTORIES, &
TRAGEDIES.

Published according to the True Originall Copies.

Martin Droeshout sculpsit London.

LONDON
Printed by Isaac Iaggard, and Ed. Blount. 1623.

William Shakespeare
April 23, 1564 - April 23, 1616

The Bard, as Shakespeare is often referred, was born in Stratford-on-Avon and baptized on April 26, 1564. His mother, Mary Arden, was related to the Ardens who held large estates in the English countryside. His father, John Shakespeare, was one of Stratford's leading citizens. He served as a leatherworker for the Queen, a member of town council and a brief term as mayor.

The Shakespeares moved up in society from tradesman to esquire when John Shakespeare was granted the arms and style of a gentleman just prior to his death in 1601.

William Shakespeare attended a local grammar school, studied rhetoric, classical literature and Christian ethics. He did not attend college but it is widely accepted that he read practically everything in print. The Gutenberg printing press had been invented only one hundred or so years earlier, so it was certainly conceivable someone could read an entire library.

Shakespeare married Ann Hathaway at the age of 18. Their daughter, Susanna, was born a year later, and twins Hamnet and Judith were born in 1585. Hamnet lived only to the age of eleven.

From 1590 to 1613 Shakespeare wrote thirty-seven plays (some scholars argue thirty-eight), helped stage his own plays, acted in small roles, helped manage an acting troupe and was part owner of the Old Globe Theatre. From 1593 - 1594, when theatres were closed because of a plague, Shakespeare wrote his narrative poetry. His plays include comedies, tragedies, histories and romances.

There is little known of Shakespeare since he did not write about himself or actually publish his plays. In fact there has been a great deal of speculation that Shakespeare did not write any of the plays attributed to him. One school of thought claims his plays were written by a wealthy lord who did not want to be associated with the theatre, while others believe his young apprentices wrote the plays.

The reasoning is: 1) He lacked a college education; 2) No manuscripts exist in his writing; 3) Little is known of his life, and; 4) No one person contains that much genius.

It is widely accepted amongst scholars and historians that Shakespeare did author the plays attributed to him. Shakespeare created his plays to be seen and did not have the time or inclination to write them out for publication. He wrote for a relatively small audience. He needed to keep adding new plays if he was to keep his theatre filled with patrons.

Shakespeare read the classics (ancient Greek and Roman comedies and tragedies), French and Italian plays, legends, folk plays, mythology, historical chronicles, and the Bible. He used every source he could find to come up with secular ideas. He would often select a plot he found elsewhere and convert it into something quite brilliant and distinctly his own.

Elizabethan Theatre

Shakespeare and his contemporaries, like today's playwrights, were not interested in telling their audiences how to live their lives. They simply wanted to paint a picture of life (the good as well as the bad) and allow the audiences to draw their own conclusions. Their work was (and is) that of painting a portrait of life, or holding up a mirror to nature, and, hopefully, entertaining us in the meantime.

The theatre was not very popular with local merchants, the Puritans, the Church and, to some degree, the government.

Local merchants were not happy with the loss of business, since all performances were at 2:00 p.m., Monday through Saturday. Merchants were also displeased with their young apprentices taking off in the middle of the day to see one of Shakespeare's comedies or tragedies.

The Puritans felt it was necessary for the stage to show only the good and holy. They feared any wrongdoing seen on the stage would be perceived as how-to-live by the audience. The church was dissatisfied with the theatre because it kept people from prayer. The government was concerned because theatres were arousing public outcries against religious and political leaders. Since sanitary conditions were pretty poor, the theatre, because of such large crowds, was a breeding place for germs and disease.

Queen Elizabeth I mandated that no theatre could perform material that had to do with contemporary religious or political figures. The Master of Revels was the official censor. Theatres also had to be licensed in order to stage plays. Because of the pressure from the merchants, it was almost impossible to receive a permit to perform in London. Most theatres were built just outside the city limits.

The church and the government had traditionally sponsored all theatrical activities. They took care of all the expenses: Performers, musicians, musical instruments, theatre rental, costumes, props, etc. But once the church and government no longer favored what the theatre was doing, their financial support was eliminated.

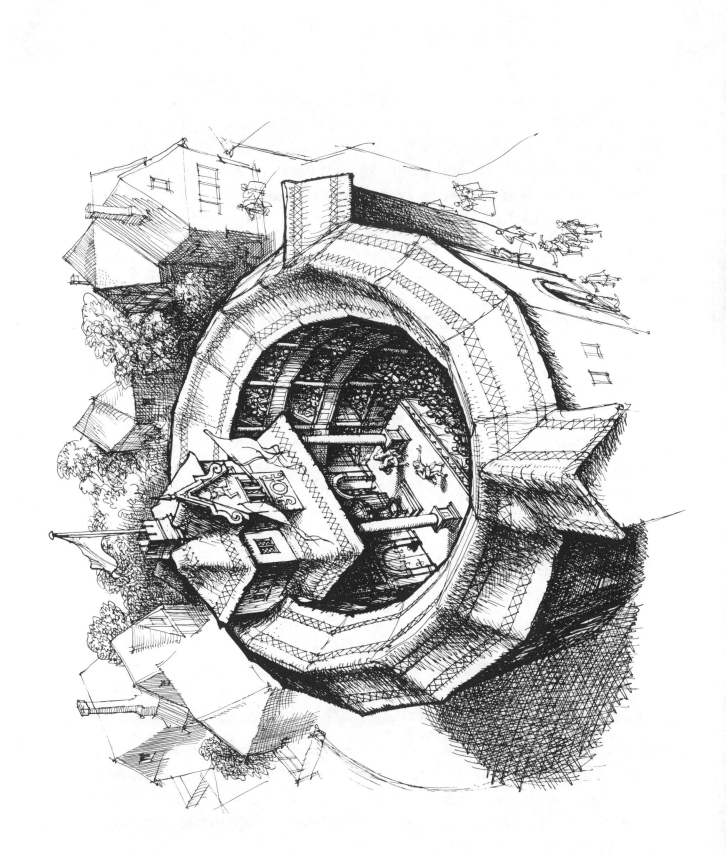

Most countries today, because of the understanding of how important it is for a society to develop and nurture art, heavily subsidize their theatres. This results in keeping the cost of tickets within reach of the poor as well as the wealthy — making the theatre accessible to everyone. The United States is one of a few countries that does relatively little in the way of subsidizing theatre or the arts.

James Burbage constructed the first Elizabethan theatre in 1576. It was simply known as the Theatre. Twenty-three years later (1599) his two sons, Richard and Cuthbart, constructed the Globe, just outside London. This is where Shakespeare produced most of his plays and became part owner.

In 1613 the Globe burned down during a performance of Henry VIII. It was rebuilt the following year and stayed up long enough to be torn down by the Puritans in 1644. Today there are efforts being made to build a replica of the Old Globe on the site where it once stood.

There are no records or drawings to tell us exactly what the Elizabethan theatres looked like. The following description is based on what historians have come to believe existed.

Actors performed on a raised platform, surrounded by the audience on three sides. Standing spectators, "groundlings," paid a penny for admission and stood in a pit in front of the stage. Those that wished to sit on seats in the surrounding galleries would pay an additional penny.

Behind the raised platform was a stage house or "tiring house." This gave the actors a place to change costumes, store props and make entrances and exits. The upstage area (located farthest from the groundlings) was known as the "inner below," and it was covered by a curtain or arras. Just above it was a balcony referred to as the "inner above." Most of the action took place on downstage area. Love scenes, i.e., the balcony scene in ROMEO AND JULIET, Kings and generals overlooking battles, and entrances of royalty would use the "inner above."

The theatre was open-air, and sun was the source of light. Unlike today's theatres, the actors and the audience members were lit. If a scene took place during the night we would be told in the dialogue, or an actor might enter with a torch.

Scenery

Shakespeare's plots moved quickly from one location to another. A few directors have attempted to stage Shakespeare's plays by building elaborate and highly realistic scenery for each scene. The problems are twofold; 1) A two-and-a-half hour play will last over five hours since more time would be spent changing scenery than actually performing. The play becomes a story about moving lumber.

The second problem has to do with dwarfing the actors. Some scenes might last only five minutes. If you bring on a beautifully crafted forest, filled with exotic trees, lush vegetation, sounds of wildlife and dazzling shafts of sunlight, the audience spends the first couple of minutes in awe of this newly arrived spectacle. By the time they take it all in, the scene is about finished and they have no idea what just took place.

The chore of establishing location is handled through dialogue and props. We learn from the characters where the action takes place. They will actually make reference to the fact they are in a bedroom chamber, a forest, country inn, etc. Props are used minimally. Actors entering the upright door during a scene in the King's chamber might carry in a throne. As they exit at the close of the scene through the upright door, actors will enter from the upleft door with a table, benches and beer mugs to create an inn.

Actors entering to start the scene will normally begin their dialogue the moment they step foot on stage - eliminating long, awkward pauses and keeping the pace moving.

All action took place in front of or above the neutral-looking arras. With no painted scenery, the only real form of spectacle was colored banners (used for royal processions or battles) and costumes.

Costumes

Costumes were, for the most part, in the contemporary Elizabethan fashion. Actors wore their own clothes unless portraying supernatural characters, i.e., witches, fairies, ghosts, etc. or different races. An actor playing a Roman character would probably wear a toga over his own clothes. Actors would enjoy taking advantage of showing off their personal wardrobes.

Acting

There were no female performers during the Elizabethan period. Acting was not a terribly respectable profession. Performers were seen as vagabonds and bums. It was bad enough that men would be allowed to behave in that fashion. If actors did not perform with a licensed company they were often hassled by authorities and thrown in prison.

Boys would apprentice with an acting company from the ages of six to fourteen. They were trained to play the female roles until they were of an age when their voices were too low to allow them to be believable, at which point they would start performing the male roles. As a result there would be very little in the way of kissing or intimacy on the Elizabethan stage.

Adult performers would learn numerous characters in a number of different plays, since they might perform three different plays during the course of a week. Actors were expected to act, sing, dance, fence and play musical instruments.

All acting companies were required by law to be sponsored by a patron whose rank was no lower than baron. Shakespeare was a member of the Lord Chamberlain's Men, eventually known as the King's Men.

Language

Shakespeare wrote in prose (common language) and blank verse (poetry that does not rhyme). The verse he worked with is known as iambic pentameter. Each line has five beats with two syllables per beat. The emphasis is usually on the second syllable.

"I <u>must</u>   be <u>gone</u>   and <u>live</u>   or <u>stay</u>   and <u>die</u>."

Because the language is so formal and because there is an absence of realistic scenery in Shakespeare's plays, his plays are not usually perceived as being realistic.

Students are often encouraged to paraphrase their reading assignments. This gives the teacher a good sense of just how much of the material the students are able to understand. Once they read the verse aloud, you might encourage them to read with an attempt to communicate what is going on (what they presented in their paraphrasing), rather than speaking as if they were reciting poetry or a foreign language.

Audience

Audiences were, in short, a rowdy bunch. The plays lasted close to three hours and there were no intermissions. Vendors would roam through the theatre selling food and ale (beer). Some historians believe audience members would actually sit right on the stage. It took skilled actors and good scripts to gain and keep the attention of the audience. Elizabethan theatres held somewhere between 1500 and 3000 spectators. Like most contemporary theatres, plays were staged as long as they attracted large audiences.

Teaching Methodologies

This manual is designed to supply educators with various methodologies in introducing Shakespeare to children. There is no one way or even just a few correct ways of working with the plays. What works for one teacher might not work for another. What works for this year's fifth graders might not work for next year's.

Once you find a methodology that works for you, we still encourage you to work with different ideas and approaches. This will keep you from becoming bored with the material (not that we have ever been known to present material that bores us). It will also help prevent you from steering your students to the same discoveries and behavior as previous groups.

When a director directs the same play year after year, s/he will eventually steer the actors (consciously or not) toward a finished product that has proven successful. While there is absolutely nothing wrong with wanting a finished product that pleases all involved, it would be detrimental to the overall experience if the participants were manipulated during the entire process.

It is important for actors (or students) to finish the process with a sense of ownership. Their creation needs to be just that, their creation. Too many of today's directors are merely puppeteers. No actor (or student) will be productive or responsive in such a relationship.

Looking at different approaches and reminding ourselves of the uniqueness of each group will allow us to establish an environment that nurtures creativity and discovery. This is a difficult concept to work with when we are so preoccupied with finished products in terms of test results. Please keep in mind that what the students will gain along the way — the intellectual and artistic stimulation, the improved skills in working cooperatively, as well as the pleasure of the experience — far outweighs how well they will fare on an exam.

Even if what you accomplish is their understanding that Shakespeare is to enjoy and not fear, you will have succeeded at what few scholars, professors, teachers and directors have been able to achieve in over four hundred years.

We recommend starting this material at fourth grade. However, we have observed successful applications as early as second grade. Obviously much depends on the students' background, the instructor's interests, and the administration's attitude towards whole-language based curriculums.

We expected to see some situations where teachers would want to work with this material in junior high school. It was quite a surprise to discover high school teachers asking how to use **Shakespeare for Children** with their students. If you find yourself in the situation where this is probably the only format that will allow you to successfully introduce your high school students to Shakespeare, you certainly won't want to offend them with the title.

One suggestion is to explain that this material was created for children and you thought they might have more fun with this than with the unedited, unillustrated and very lengthy version you normally work with. We don't encourage talking down to a child at any age, so we certainly wouldn't want a high-schooler to be or feel patronized.

All students need to be in possession of the text. Many will follow along with the reading (even if they are being read to) and most will appreciate the opportunity to take time experiencing the illustrations. For the younger student this will help reinforce that the material they are working with is from a book and that book (that experience) is accessible. (This is why great storytellers will have a book in hand, even if the story is committed to memory.)

Seating arrangements can be left as normal, but we encourage creating a special or different arrangement to help reinforce how special this unit is. You might have the students form a circle with their desks or be seated on the floor. Milder climates might consider a few lessons out on the lawn.

The first session in a new seating arrangement might prove somewhat distracting at the start. If you choose to rearrange your students, it would be helpful to set them up in the new seating arrangement to conduct a related lesson just prior to working with the text.

If the students will be doing the reading, and you prefer they read in front of the group, a horseshoe seating arrangement works quite nicely with the readers standing (or seated) at the opening of the shoe.

We recommend lessons of approximately forty-five minutes. You have the option of working with anywhere from six to fifteen sessions. The authors, of course, recommend using as many of these sessions as time permits. If you are not able to conduct five sessions in one week, then do as many as you can. It could prove counterproductive to do only one or two sessions each week.

Preparation

Your first assignment is to learn about Shakespeare, the period and the specific play you are teaching. Use the bibliography and your local librarian to come up with sources. There is no need to become expert in the Elizabethan period. You want enough information to help the students get a nice sense of what life was like when Shakespeare wrote his plays. You may even discover a relationship between the time and the particular play, i.e., political or religious circumstances.

Several weeks before involving the students ask them what they know about Shakespeare, the Elizabethan period and the play in study. List all they know or ask them to make their own list on a sheet of paper that you will collect. Advise them that they will be learning more about the subject in the next week or two.

One week prior to involving the students you will want to bring something in every day that is related to Shakespeare, the period and/or the play. Create a special area to post your photo, article, costume piece, stage prop, etc. (A map of England and any location mentioned in the play would be very useful.) This will help pique the students' curiosity and stir their interest.

Your first week (working with students) is spent with the students researching the period the first half of the week. Break them up into five groups and assign each group a research topic, i.e.,

1) Religion and attitude of religious leaders toward the theatre;

2) Politics and attitude of political leaders toward the theatre;

3) Elizabethan theatres, The King's Men and audiences;

4) Elizabethan costumes; and

5) Shakespeare's life (birth, schooling, parents, likes, why turn to playwriting, success, death, etc.).

You could start this week by having a dozen or so reference books available for the students to peruse. Explain that these sources are to help them get started but they will need to seek out other sources from their school and local libraries.

Give each group a list of what the entire class is researching. Explain they are to keep their eyes open for material for the other groups. When the group exploring Elizabethan theatres happens to find information about government restrictions on where theatres can be located and the type of plays that can be staged, they will offer that source to the group researching Elizabethan politics. Emphasize the thrust is to help one another rather than compete with each other.

Please give sufficient notice to librarians and parents. Send them a brief note (especially if the study of Shakespeare is new to the level you work with) advising them of the project and what sort of information the students will be seeking. With enough notice your local librarians might be able to come up with additional books. Parents may even pick up a copy of the play - in the case of students not being able to keep their text.

The first half of the week is spent with students working in their groups without supervision. It will be enough for you to walk around the room to listen to their discussions and praise them for the material they found, ability to work together, and any other positive behavior you note. Playing some Elizabethan-type music in the background would be an excellent way to help give a sense of the period as well as show how non-threatening an experience this unit is.

There may be a need to gently help an especially introverted student be able to contribute ideas or the need to pull in the reins on a particularly extroverted student so others can contribute.

After two or three days of group research, give the students time to determine how they will present their findings to the class. You may determine that the only requirement is that each person in the group present some information. Who presents what, in what order, standing or seated, at their desks or in front of the class, etc. is left to them.

The next step, of course, is for the students to present their findings to the rest of the class. You might want to use a section of blackboard to jot down significant/relevant material and leave it up a day or two or through the entire period of studying the play. Once the students have finished their presentations, you might show a film or video tape on the period. (Please check the bibliography for catalogues that supply such material.) This will permit the noting of new information or praising them for how much of the information (in the film) they discovered on their own.

First Day with the Text

When the students arrive at class, you could have the names of all the characters and locations listed on the blackboard or on large sheets of paper. These names could remain all through the study of the play. In the case of ROMEO AND JULIET you might want to divide the names up according to the Capulet and Montague families.

Arrange the students in their new seating configuration and pass out the text. Explain whether or not they can keep the text and whether or not they can write/color in it. Let them know how you plan to introduce this play to them, i.e., you will be reading it, they will volunteer to read parts, you will both read, etc.

The students could be given a moment or two to read the back cover and glance through the book. Briefly discuss the nature of tragedy.

Read the "Welcome…" on page x and go over the correct pronunciation of names. It would probably be beneficial to have the students repeat the names with you a few times.

You are now ready to study the play with your students. For the novice this can easily be a time of high anxiety. Let us take a moment to reassure you how much success we have observed as early as second grade with teachers that had absolutely no background with Shakespeare. Those of you that had the luxury of time, or an old enough group of students, to follow our recommended research preparation, will undoubtedly note how much enthusiasm the students radiate. They should be anticipating a fun and non-threatening experience. So should you!

This is an excellent time to remind yourself that your students perceive you as an authority. Don't apologize for not sharing their perception or feel the nagging need to tell them you have never done this before. Keep a smile on your face, don't rush them or yourself, maintain flexibility (hopefully you will have enough time to avoid the need to stick to a rigid lesson-plan) and you will be great!

Who does the reading and how much is read at one time is entirely up to you. We will list here a number of options. All methods have proven successful. Your particular goals and your students' capabilities will determine which option you select.

The seven options are not listed in order of preference and they certainly are not the only options available.

Options

OPTION #1: Seek volunteers to read characters for the entire first act. You will also need a volunteer to read the prologue and be the narrator. (Keep a record of who reads to make sure everyone has had a chance over the next week.) It is perfectly acceptable for young ladies to read male roles and vice versa.

At the end of each scene ask the readers to have a seat so everyone can discuss what the scene was about. Make sure they cover all important elements of plot. It helps to go through each page and ask them to paraphrase sections you suspect they might not be clear about.

In some situations students will stop periodically to seek clarification. You will have to use your own discretion with this one. Do you wait until the end of the scene before they ask questions, the end of the page or when they have the question? If it appears there is mass confusion, you will probably want to keep the plot clear from page-to-page. Flow and continuity are important, but understanding the story is more important.

We suggest using the discussion period strictly to keep the plot clear. More probing questions can be explored after the play's conclusion.

Once you are satisfied the students are clear about the scene, ask your readers to continue with the next scene. Throughout the entire process, remind yourself how important positive reinforcement is. Find any and every opportunity at your disposal to praise their contributions. Even if words aren't appropriate, you can always nod or smile or lift one of those all-approving eyebrows.

When you are asking questions to see how well the students are following the plot, try to avoid the need for them to give you ONLY the answer you are seeking. An excellent example was demonstrated in a group of fourth graders we observed. At the end of Act I, when Romeo and Juliet appear to be falling in love, the teacher asked, "What is the problem we discover in this act?"

What the teacher wanted to hear was related to how the two young lovers belong to feuding families and that may prevent them from coming together. What she heard was:

1. Capulets and Montagues fought in the street.

2. Juliet is supposed to marry someone she never met.

3. Juliet is supposed to marry Paris.

4. Romeo believes something bad is going to happen.

5. Tybalt wants to kill Romeo.

6. Tybalt's uncle won't let Tybalt fight with Romeo.

7. Romeo and his friends went to a party they weren't invited to.

The teacher responded to each of the above with, "No, that is not the problem I am thinking of." The point is that each of those responses is correct. Rather than encouraging the students to think for themselves, that teacher was encouraging them to think the way she does. She expressed absolutely no appreciation for their insights, willingness to share, recollections and reactions.

This teacher started out with twenty-two highly enthused and self-motivated students. By the third day the students began to quiet down for fear of failure (to come up with the "correct" response). The teacher was frustrated because of such poor participation in discussions and it was difficult for the teacher to assess whether or not the students were following the story.

OPTION #2: Seek volunteers for each scene (as opposed to the entire act). Ask them to read the scene before the entire group and carry on your discussion at the conclusion. After discussion, seek volunteers to read the next scene.

OPTION #3: Volunteers read each scene/act and you read the narration. This allows you to participate as well as add a more dramatic/interpretive dimension.

OPTION #4: This is usually reserved for the very young students. Here we have the teacher doing all the reading. You will probably find yourself stopping at the end of each page to discuss what has just happened. Remember to allow them to carry on a majority of the discussion.

OPTION #5: Rarely will you find a shortage of students willing to volunteer to read. It is important not to draft your readers. This, as you are well aware of, can be devastating. If, early on, there is some resistance to reading, you can divide the students so the young men read all the male roles and the young women read all the female roles.

OPTION #6: Write names of characters on sheets of paper and have the students select names (without knowing who they are choosing). You may or may not wish to have them draw from the correct gender. This can be done by scene or act. The former will eat up a lot of time but helps keep them involved.

OPTION #7: Divide the students into five (5) groups. Have group one read the first act silently, group two read the second act silently, etc. When they are finished ask them to determine who will read which character for the class. (Prior to putting them in their groups, you would do well to have them discuss how to solve the problem of more than one person *wanting* to read the same character.)

The students are also asked to determine what the scene is about so they can tell the class (in their own words) before they actually read each scene.

Second Day with the Text

Post a quote from the act you are about to study. You may do this because of the potential for discussion or because of the imagery in the language.

Start the period by going over what the students remember of Act I. Once you feel they covered the essential plot ingredients move on to reading the second act.

OPTION #1: Repeat the same process as day 1.

OPTION #2: Select one of the other options listed for the first day. You would head in this direction if you weren't satisfied with the first day's work or if you simply wish to create a change that might keep the students more (or equally) involved.

Third Day with the Text

Post your quote and start the period by going over what the students remember of Act II. Once you feel they covered the essential plot ingredients, move on to reading the third act.

Fourth Day with the Text *

ACT IV

* If necessary, it is all right to combine Acts IV and V on the fourth day.

Fifth Day with the Text

ACT V

Sixth Day with the Text

Start the period by going over what is remembered from Act V. Once you feel the students have covered the essential plot ingredients, move on to discussion of the play.

Themes

Asking a typical college student to identify a theme is like pulling teeth (If you can pull a tooth from a cucumber!). They are convinced 1) there can be only one right answer or 2) they lack the perception to provide an acceptable response. A theme is the main topic, central idea or message. Typically they are implicit (implied) rather than explicit (actually stated). *The Wizard of OZ* is a perfect example of a piece of work that actually states a potential theme in the text, i.e., "There is no place like home." Another theme can be seen in how many characters are searching for a certain characteristic, i.e., courage or compassion, and discover it isn't necessary to go outside themselves to find or develop that characteristic. Laura Ingalls Wilder's autobiographical stories share the common theme of the struggles of life on the frontier. The point is, before you ask your student to identify possible themes, use literature they are all familiar with to define and explore the concept.

To What Degree do I Need to Control the Discussion?

The age, background, attitude and interests of your students will determine (to a large degree) the direction of your discussion. Students do have the potential to go on endlessly about absolutely nothing, but when you get a sense they really do have a contribution to make, go with it as long as you can. Use this opportunity to ask students to respond to each other. "Has anyone else ever experienced... Does anyone else know anyone like...?" This may mean eliminating some of the questions we intended to ask but, hey, by now we have all learned to compromise.

Praise Praise Praise

Most teachers not only understand this next idea, they practice it religiously. Please look for opportunities to express your appreciation whenever students contribute ideas, use their imagination or simply listen to you or their peers. (Please see page 96.) So many of us in education expect students to respect us, yet we rarely reciprocate. Let us make a conscious effort to vocalize before the entire class our appreciation for the students able or willing to contribute to the process. This mutual respect (where we don't talk down to them but with them) works miracles. The end result is students moan and groan when it's time to leave class and knock the doors down when it's time to start the next class.

So, with that bit of pontification out of the way, let us get on to possible discussion questions. Use what you feel is appropriate, don't weigh yourself down with expectations, create a relaxed environment (maybe a new seating arrangement) and have fun. (This doesn't have to be a job. It can be quite enjoyable. Your enthusiasm will be highly contagious.)

Discussion Questions

What do you know about Shakespeare and Elizabethan England?

Do you think Shakespeare would have made a good friend? Why?

Why do you think Shakespeare wrote this play?

If Shakespeare were alive, why might he want us to see this play?

Why do you think theaters have been staging this play for hundreds of years?

Why do you think audiences come to see this play more than once?

What was it in the play that made you happy?

Was there anything in the play that made you sad?

Can you identify the different emotions experienced by characters in the play?

Can you tell us which of those emotions you have experienced?

What do you see as the major ideas expressed in the play?

What lessons do you think Shakespeare wanted his audience to walk away with?

What were some of the things that happened in the play that you liked *and* disliked?

Which characters did you like? (And why?)

Which characters did you feel the least sympathy towards? (And why?)

Are there any characters you would like to emulate as you grow up?

Pick one character you would like to live with and tell me why.

Pick one character and imagine s/he is with us today. What type of music, food, clothes, car, etc. would s/he like and why?

How can you learn more about Shakespeare and/or his plays?

Why is it important to study Shakespeare and see his plays ?

What is the difference between watching a live play and a movie? What are the advantages/disadvantages of each? Why would it be a good idea to see a live play once in awhile?

If Shakespeare were here, what would you like to tell or ask him?

If you were to tell a parent what you liked most about this play, what would that be?

Why would you recommend your best friend read this play?

If you were to rewrite the play, what would you change? Would you add or remove any characters? Would you change how they related to one another? Would you change the ending?

Would you like to perform this play? If so, which character(s) would you like to play and why?

If we were to stage the play, do you foresee any problems or difficulties?

If you were to write a play (about anything or anyone you want) what would you write about? What would you want your audience to think or feel as they left the theater?

Have you ever attended live theater? What did you like or dislike about your experience?

What type of behavior is expected of audience members in live theater?

How is that behavior different than, say, attending a ball game or a concert?

Are you glad we studied this play? Why or why not?

What else would you like us to study or explore?

Values

After discussing/defining values ask your students to list values embraced by certain characters and find out whether or not students share those values. Some values to consider include:

1. Being responsible
2. Emotional support
3. Respect for others
4. Happy marriage/family unit
5. Living up to potential
6. Honesty
7. Earning a good living
8. Helping others
9. Freedom (of...)
10. Non-judgemental
11. Patience
12. Forgiveness
13. Democracy
14. Education
15. Religion
16. Cleanliness
17. Privacy
18. Charity
19. Commitment to community
20. Women's liberation

Depending on the age of your students, the game *Scruples* is a wonderful tool to create a dialogue surrounding values. It is crucial the students don't find themselves criticized for their response, but use their response as an opportunity for discussion/exploration. The more courageous teachers will participate in the game.

It might prove useful to look at both sides of a value and explore the consequences of having/not having these values, i.e., responsibility vs. irresponsibility or charity vs. miserliness. Ultimately we discover we are accountable for our actions.

Wait-Time in Asking Questions

It is such a frustrating experience to observe teachers work with a Shakespeare unit where there is insufficient wait-time when asking questions. It seems that most teachers were all too willing to call on the first person to raise a hand - especially if that first person doesn't usually participate.

Please take plenty of time before calling on someone. Some students, as we all know, are very shy and slow to involve themselves. If we continue to seek a response immediately after asking the question, the shy or less assertive student eventually learns not to think for him/herself because someone else will come up with the answer.

Repeat the question a few times and take a few pauses. It is such a wonderful feeling to ask a question, see a couple of hands raised, ask the question again and see a few more hands come up, ask the question again and the entire class is eager to respond.

Do your best to avoid the temptation of answering your own questions. If a response is not clear or not headed in the direction you wish, express your appreciation for the contribution and seek alternative responses/reactions.

Journal

During the week you work with the text you could ask the students to make journal entries at the end of each session.

Tell them exactly what you want them to include. Some suggestions are: 1) important elements of the plot; 2) what they liked about the act; 3) what they didn't like about the act; 4) characters they felt sympathetic toward (and why); 5) what they think the next act will deal with; 6) new words they learned; and 7) characters they didn't like (and why); etc.

An interesting idea for you to consider is the incorporation of a GROUP JOURNAL. Depending on the sort of group activity you have designed and how often the students change groups, you can have them make an entry at the end of each scene. Ask them to simply write a few sentences to describe the action of the scene in study. All the sentences will be read in sequence at the end of the play. This same exercise can be done with individual journal entries.

Warm-up Activities

There are a number of reasons why a brief warm-up would be helpful: You might be teaching this unit just following P.E. and a bit of centering might be in order; you might be working at the end of the day when students' energy level is low or their thoughts are elsewhere; you might be working in a situation where the students are not accustomed to working together; or you might wish to reinforce how unique and non-threatening this new unit is.

Whatever your reason, please keep in mind these are just a few suggestions. Use them as they are laid out or use them to come up with activities more appropriate for your students.

CREATIVE DRAMA (Cottrell), THE NEW GAMES BOOK (Fluegelman), and IMPROVISATION FOR THE THEATER (Spolin) contain volumes of excellent ideas. One of the more attractive elements of these activities (and those found in the books listed above) is their ability to bring children together regardless of the different physical, intellectual or social development found within the group.

Warm-up #1

Divide the class into small groups (four to six per group). Assign each group the same letter or word. (The word should be from the play you are studying.) Ask the students to use their bodies (standing, seated or lying down) to form the letter/word. They make all the decisions and the only rule is that each person in the group is to participate.

Once complete, each group is to show the class their letter/ word. Point out how many different ways there are to create the same letter/word and that each choice is correct AND interesting.

Explain this is what is meant by using our imagination. Once you start your discussion of the play, point out how many different and interesting ways they came up with to write a letter/ word and that our discussion is no different. You are asking them to use their imagination and there can never be a wrong answer.

Warm-up #2

(They will want to do this one every day - and that's probably OK.)

Divide the students into small groups (changing the composition of the group each day). One volunteer from each group comes to you with pencil and paper. The group of volunteers are given the same word that they are to draw for their group. They are not permitted to speak or write letters when they draw.

Once the volunteers are given the word, they are to return to their group and wait for the signal to begin drawing. When all groups have determined the word, ask for a new volunteer from each group and repeat the process.

Now, what words do I use? If you want the drawing to relate to the play, you might make selections from what you are about to read, i.e., you are about to study Act I, Scene 1 from ROMEO AND JULIET, so you have selected rapier, death, mask, cupid, torch and Prince (since you have six students in each group and you will want each to have an opportunity to draw).

It would be helpful for you to inform the class they will be drawing words selected from the play or they will be drawing adjectives, verbs, sports, moods, occupations, fruit, vegetables, modes of transportation, etc. Emphasize how one needn't be good at drawing to be successful. Be sure to seek VOLUNTEERS for all activities.

Warm-up #3

This activity is not (directly) related to your Shakespeare unit but children (and adults!) will love it. We suggest you give it a try and then determine what, if any, value this will have for your group.

??? Who Started the Motion ???

One VOLUNTEER steps out of the room and the rest of the class stands in a circle at arm's width. Someone in the circle VOLUNTEERS to be the leader. The leader then proceeds to start a simple movement that everyone else will duplicate. The volunteer now returns to the room and stands directly in the center of the circle.

At this point the volunteer is standing in the middle of a bunch of students all making the same movement patterns. The leader is to change the movement every thirty seconds or so. The rest of the circle is to repeat those movements as they change.

The object is for the person standing in the center of the circle to determine who is initiating the movement. The volunteer is given three guesses. If you have a large class, you might try this in two circles or have one half watch as the others work. Let the students determine who it is that must step out of the circle next.

Warm-up #4

This idea works best after the third or fourth day with the text. Seat the students in a circle on the floor. The person that volunteers to be "it" is to walk around the entire group three times then sit in his/her original spot.

While "it" walks the 100-yard dash in ten seconds, those seated are to take turns saying something related to the play. It could be the name of a character, a location in the play, a quote from the play, a prop, anything.

The idea is that those seated will come up with something (one-at-a-time and in order) before "it" can be seated. Let the students decide how to determine who will be "it" next.

Warm-up #5

Pass the Mask

The group is on their feet in a circle. One person volunteers to start the activity. The volunteer (A) simply passes a mask (facial expression) to the person to the left (B). B duplicates the mask and passes it back to A. Now B passes a new mask to the person to his/her left (C). C duplicates mask given by B and passes the duplication back to B and sends the next person (D) a new mask. The process repeats itself around the entire circle.

Pass the Sound

Go through the same process as above, only now a novel sound is made. A new volunteer starts the process and instead of passing to the left, pass to the right.

Pass the Movement

Same process as above.

Pass the Movement and Sound

Same process as above.

Pass the Fruit/Ball/Garden Tool/etc.

Same process as above.

Warm-up #6

Now our passing game becomes a bit more complicated. The group passes an idea, attitude or expression without sound or physical contact. The idea, however, is not to change what you receive, but keep the SAME MESSAGE going around the circle. So if the volunteer passes a sad farewell, using a sad-looking expression and very slow wave of the hand, we want to see if the same message is passed AND RECEIVED by the time it gets to the last two in the circle.

We add an interesting element, not seen in warm-up #5. The only person to see what is passed is the person actually receiving the message. Everyone is standing with their backs to the circle. When a person is about to pass a message, they tap the person next to them on the shoulder, the person tapped now turns towards the center of the circle and faces the person about to pass a message. Once you pass the message, you can watch the rest of the events. When the activity is complete, have everyone watch how the last person sends a message and then have the person that started the activity demonstrate what s/he did.

It would be a very rare situation where the message does not change. Be careful the students don't find a person to "blame" for the change. Use this to discuss how important it is for us to "listen" with our eyes (to interpret) and then "speak" with our bodies (to communicate). The value of non-verbal communication is clearly demonstrated. You can also discuss what else they learned/discovered, what they liked/disliked, etc.

Warm-up #7

Developing Trust

Students not accustomed to reading, or expressing ideas before you or their peers, need to know they can trust one another. The next couple of warm-ups will help to that end.

The Circle will not be Unbroken

Students stand close to one another in a circle. A volunteer stands in the middle of the circle. The volunteer closes his/her eyes as the students in the circle GENTLY move the volunteer in different configurations around the circle. The group is to help the volunteer keep his/her heels in the same spot. The point is for the volunteer to experience a sense of falling as s/he discovers the group will protect him/her. The teacher will allow this to go on for a minute or so before switching volunteers.

The volunteer is NOT to wear glasses or dangly jewelry. Female students are to stand in the center of the circle with their arms folded across their chest (right hand holding on to left shoulder and left hand holding on to right shoulder) and male students are to stand with the arms down to their side. Remind those in the circle to rotate gently.

This is an excellent exercise in helping diffuse gender or racial barriers.

Warm-up #8

Not Seeing is Believing

Divide the students into pairs. (This is a great opportunity to put people together that normally tend to avoid one another.) Hand one person in each pair a blindfold and ask them to secure it to their partner. (If the person being blindfolded wears glasses, be sure the glasses are brought along.)

Explain to the sighted partner where s/he is to lead the "blind" partner, e.g. the water-fountain on the second floor in the building across the track field. Encourage them to take their time and never lose sight (!) of the fact their partner is "blind." Physical contact must be maintained the entire time.

Once they reach their destination, they switch roles and return to the class. This provides an excellent opportunity to get better acquainted with students, to develop trust, to discuss the obstacles/concerns of someone really blind, to understand how other senses are affected and to point out what each of them did that proved to be helpful in getting someone to their destination.

This is a fun exercise and it certainly gets the rest of the school curious about this unit. Please be sure to follow along with them on their "blind" excursion. Coach them as they walk through the building/grounds, reminding them their objective is to help their partner. There is nothing like incorporating a steel beam between two doors into the exercise because the sighted person may be more concerned with watching his peers than his partner.

Warm-up #9

Observation Skills

Divide the class into groups of four. Each group is to be seated on the floor in their own space. A volunteer is selected in each group and sits in front of the three others in the group.

The three members are to spend the next two minutes closely observing the volunteer. When the two minutes are up, have the three turn their backs to the volunteer. The volunteer will now change three things about his/her attire. When each of the volunteers has completed the three changes, have the group turn around and see how long it takes for them to determine what three items were changed.

Once this is completed, have each group select another volunteer to be observed. The students, once again, have two minutes to observe the new volunteer. This time the volunteer is asked to change four things about his/her attire.

Repeat the process as long as you wish and determine how many items are to be changed.

Warm-up #10

Hearing Our Environment

(More observation skills)

Ask the entire class to lie on their backs with their heads towards the center of a circle. They are to close their eyes and (without saying anything) simply listen to the sounds in their environment. Explain that after a few minutes you will call on them to identify the sources of those sounds.

Once they have identified the sounds, select specific sounds and ask them to use their imaginations to decide what else those sounds might be.

Now comes the fun part. Your homework is to bring in a dozen or so items from home/office. With the students' eyes still closed, make the sounds of each item, asking them determine what the actual item is and then what the actual item might be - being as imaginative as they can.

Warm-up #11

Developing Compassion

Ask the students to help you list on the board the various emotions / personality types found in the play you are studying. Divide the students in half so one half watches the other half play.

Students are to move about the room as if they were experiencing each emotion / personality you select. They are not to speak or make physical contact. Once you have gone through an emotion, ask those watching to comment on how many different ways there were to express anger, joy, etc.

Now the two groups switch. This time do not allow the observers to know which emotion/personality is assigned to those on their feet. Once the group is done, ask the class to identify the emotion. Have the group walk with that emotion once again and this time, as they are walking, have them (or the observers) come up with a sentence or two that might be spoken from someone walking/looking like that.

Warm-up #12

Stretching the Imagination

(You will want to wait on this one until the class is very comfortable with you, each other and possibly with looking foolish before their peers.)

Two volunteers come before the entire class. You can set them up in any physical arrangement you wish. They will immediately begin a dialogue that makes sense out of that physical arrangement. We discover in the dialogue what their relationship is to one another and where the scene takes place.

An example would be to put a chair behind and next to a desk. Seat one person in the chair behind the desk and ask the other to approach the empty seat. It is up to them to start a dialogue/ relationship once the student reaches the empty seat. They are not given time to plan or discuss the activity. You might have one person standing on the desk and the other walk into the classroom. One could be under the desk as the other walks in or they can both be seated back-to-back on the floor.

The choices you make are unending and their choices are often fascinating. Be sure to use only volunteers and point out how important it is they listen to what happens and not go into the situation already deciding what the place and relationship is. They need to understand that the place can be anywhere, not just the classroom.

Warm-up #13

Pantomime

Explain that the meaning of pantomime is essentially communicating without words and that we are about to try some pantomime exercises. Divide the class into groups of five to eight students. You will give the group an activity to pantomime and those watching are to determine what that activity is.

Let the students know the categories you are working with, i.e., movies, books, cities in your state, a Shakespearean play (you will want to list a dozen or so on the board), sporting event, etc.

Give each group their pantomime and approximately ten minutes to work on it. Allow the discussion to take any direction the students wish. You could begin by asking them to comment on frustrations, successes, or what it might be like to live among the world of the mute and never be able to express yourself with words.

Warm-up #14

Energy Pick-er-upper

You will need plenty of wide-open space for this one. No walls, chairs, desks, etc. One half of the class will participate while the other half watches. You will want to switch groups at the end.

At one end of the room sits a lonely chair or bench. Students lineup at the other end - at least eight feet in front of a wall. (A padded wall is desirable. No wall is preferable.) A volunteer (V) agrees to be "it." The person that is "it" is given an eraser.

V is to touch someone in the line with the eraser. V then runs to the bench, puts the eraser on it and runs back to the line. The object is for the person tagged to pick the eraser up (after it is placed on the bench) and tag V with it - before V crosses the line of students.

If V tosses the eraser to the bench and the eraser falls, V is to start over. Whenever you have a V that never seems to make it past the line, you will probably want to set a limit on how many times V will have to be "it".

This exercise gets the ol' adrenaline flowing, gives students an opportunity to burn off some energy and allows them to demonstrate how cunning they can be.

Warm-up #15

Stretching Exercises

Select activities that you feel will best allow students to release tension and limber up. There is no correct way to do the following. You can make your own suggestions. We do, however, advise against making a specific suggestion and then demonstrating. The students, especially the younger ones, will be more concerned with duplicating what you did in order to do it correctly or to not be required to think for themselves.

FIRECRACKERS

      SEEDS GROWING

           POPCORN POPPING

              RUBBER BANDS

AWAKENING

    TAFFY

      FLOATING FEATHERS

          WALKING A TIGHTROPE

WALKING IN MUD

   SAND

    HOT WATER

     COLD WATER

      DAMP GRASS

      BLACK OIL

As they go through the process take time to remind them of texture, weight, smell, pain, comfort, temperature, sounds, what else it might remind them of, etc.

Activities Across the Curriculum

Most likely you will be introducing **Shakespeare for Children** in your Language Arts, Reading or Literature class. However, we see the value of integrating themes or topics across the curriculum. If children see that a theme has relevance to every curricular subject area, they will be able to see the world holistically; a world that is interactive and integrated, not separate and segregated. Children will look to all the subject areas as holding keys for the solution to problems. They will look upon learning as on-going and unified, rather than segmented into discrete subjects and activities.

What follows are some suggestions for integrating the study of Shakespeare throughout the curriculum. We hope that you consider these suggestions as just that: SUGGESTIONS. We believe every teacher has a vast storehouse of ideas and must be creative, many times out of necessity. So, we ask that you consider our ideas as a means to motivate numerous ideas of your own that relate to your particular class, grade level, physical environment, experiential background, etc.

The suggested activities we outline here pertain to creative writing, art, music, theatre, social studies, science, mathematics and physical education.

Creative Writing Activities

Re-writing in Today's Vernacular

Divide the students into their groups and assign them short phrases from the scene/act you just studied. Ask them to rewrite the phrase as they would speak it in today's vernacular.

*   *   *   *   *

Re-writing as Shakespeare Might

Divide the students into their groups and assign them short phrases from today's vernacular, i.e., it is raining, I am hungry, I miss you, I would like to travel on a spaceship, etc. and ask them to word it as Shakespeare might.

Elizabethan Newspaper

Have groups select categories they will write, i.e., sports, business, entertainment, who's who, comics, classified, editorial page, front page, "Dear Willie" (?), etc. Someone might even write an ad for the Old Globe for whichever play you are studying.

Give the groups time to work together and eventually help them cut out their articles and paste them up for an actual newspaper. Either your students or students from an art class could come up with any graphics/drawings. (This is a great way to engage other teachers/students and stir up school-wide interest in your project.)

Your school or some of your students may have access to computers with graphic capabilities. A local print shop might even be willing to run off copies for your class or the school especially if you design an Elizabethan-looking ad for them.

Emotions

HAPPINESS is an emotion most of us would want to experience.

1) Select a character from the first act that you wish was happier.

2) Describe what you might do to help that person feel that way.

3) Select a popular television or sports figure.

4) Write three reasons that person might not be happy.

5) Write what you might do for each of those reasons to make this person happy.

*　　　*　　　*　　　*　　　*

What happens to us when we feel ANGER? How do we experience it in our bodies and in our hearts? Select a character from any of the acts that is feeling anger. Why is that person angry and what could s/he do to eliminate that anger? Was it necessary for the character to respond in a way that allowed the anger to develop? How else could that person have responded? Who, then, has control over our emotions? Write situations that have made you angry and explain how you might have selected a response other than anger.

Summarizing Each Scene

Write a summary of each scene in your own words. This exercise can be done individually or in a group.

*　　　*　　　*　　　*　　　*

Time Machine

Imagine you were sent back to the 14th century (or whenever the play takes place). Describe your experience in a letter to your best friend. Be sure to include what you like about your visit as well as what you do not like.

*   *   *   *   *

Elopement (the lovers)

Pretend you are Romeo or Juliet and you just ran away from home. Write a letter to a parent.

Elopement (the parent)

You are a parent of Romeo or Juliet and they ran away from home one year ago today. Write your son/daughter a letter.

Character Time Capsule

Think about the possessions that are important to you. Do any of those possessions become more or less important as time goes by. Select five items that would be of lasting significance to you and place them in a time capsule to be seen five hundred years from now. Write a couplet (two-line rhyming poem) to accompany each item.

Think about the possessions that are important to your favorite character in a play. Select five items that would be of lasting significance to him/her and place them in a time capsule to be seen five hundred years from then. Write a couplet to accompany each item.

Interview

You are a newspaper reporter for your local/school paper and are given the assignment to interview a personality in the time of Shakespeare. Select one of the following individuals and then list all the questions you would like to ask.

This can be done by having one student serve as the reporter with another as the individual being interviewed. Or you might have the student conducting the interview actually respond from the perspective of the person being interviewed.

1. Your character in the play (for those acting out the play).

2. William Shakespeare.

3. Richard Burbage (famous Shakespearean actor).

4. A boy playing the role of Juliet at the Globe Theatre in 1603.

5. A stagehand at the Old Globe in 1603 - would probably play a minor role.

Playbill

One or two students develop a playbill (theatre program).

Consider incorporating the following information:

1. Cover design. (Include date, place and name of theatre.)

2. Plot summary.

3. List of characters/performers.

4. List of designers/technicians.

5. List of support staff (publicity, box office, ushers, etc.)

6. Acknowledgments - individuals and businesses that donated time/material.

Computer graphics would also come in handy with the playbill.

Art Activities

#1

Assign each of the five groups a different act from the play. Each group member is then assigned a scene from that act. Their responsibility is to draw a picture that best expresses the action of that scene.

It helps to select one color for the Capulets' clothing, one for the Montagues' and a third for those not related. It is also useful to have the students choose hair designs and colors for "Romeo" and "Juliet" that remain constant in all groups.

During the time allotted for drawing you will want to circulate amongst the students and praise them for their creations. You might ask them what scene they are drawing, what is going on in the scene, where the scene takes place and maybe suggest a few details that will help bring the environment/situation to life. The important point here is to engage the students.

When individuals finish their scene, casually bring them together as you discuss the play, the book, their experience, etc.

Eventually you will post all of the drawings (in order of how they appear in the play) and look at the play from that perspective. You can take the students through each picture and ask the artists how they came up with their idea.

You might even post the drawings along a hallway. This will create interest and curiosity throughout the school.

#2

Design a new cover for the SHAKESPEARE FOR CHILDREN book you are working with and include one line from the play.

#3

Distribute copies of page 76 and ask your students to draw a picture and select a line from the play that relates to what you believe the play is all about. Eventually they will duplicate their creation (with a fabric crayon) on a T-shirt.

#4

Divide the students into groups. Each group is assigned a scene from Act I. They are to create a pose they feel best represents the scene. Give them plenty of time to work on their 'painting' and eventually they will show the class.

The class can try to determine which scene is being represented and discussion can take on any direction you/they wish. (A Polaroid camera will add a whole new dimension to this exercise.)

Bring in a few paintings (that include people) from the Elizabethan period (or the period of the play). Based on the students' knowledge of that time, ask them to bring the people in the paintings to life.

Here are a few areas they might explore:

Where they are.

Why are they there.

What is their relationship to one another.

What do they do for a living.

What is their favorite character in the play and why.

What are they saying to each other.

If they were to walk away, where would they go and what would the rest of their day be like.

Describe their home, family, religion, recreational activities, etc.

Art-related question:

Why do you think the author of **Shakespeare for Children: The Story of Romeo and Juliet** wanted the first illustration in the book to also be the last illustration?

Acting Activity

Presenting a Monologue

Assign students to put to memory a short phrase of their choosing (no more than two minutes long). Have them present their monologue to the class. Discussion can springboard into why they selected that phrase, how they went about memorizing, obstacles actors might have in memorizing an entire script, value of paraphrasing before memorizing, what an actor considers when delivering a line, etc.

Music Activities

Instruments

Students could research the different types of musical instruments used during the period of the play. They could draw or recreate examples of such instruments. You might also find people who know about or even play these instruments and use them as a class resource. Contemporary recordings of these instruments may be available. A music department of a local university or library would certainly be of help.

Themes

After reading the play, have the students listen to the theme from a movie version of the play. Ask them to write their own lyrics for the theme.

Opera

Older students might select to recall the opera version of ROMEO AND JULIET by Gounod.

Elizabethan Jam Session

Students could create/borrow instruments and play background music for each scene. Discussion could evolve around what criteria they used to determine instruments and tempo.

Social Studies

Another Time and Place

Students could rewrite sections of the play reflecting different cultures or historical periods. For example, how would HAMLET be different if it occurred in a traditional Mayan cultural setting? How would HAMLET be different if it occurred two hundred years from now?

Another example would be to rewrite ROMEO AND JULIET to reflect the Montagues and Capulets being from families on opposite sides during the Civil War or from families in your own city at this particular time.

Timeline

A timeline of a Shakespearean play could be put on the wall, then students could research important historical events during the period the play is set and add them to the timeline.

Dioramas

Students could build dioramas of scenes from the play concentrating on the authenticity of building structure, clothing, weapons, etc. A study of such cultural characteristics could precede the diorama-building.

Now and Then

Students could contrast the present-day geography, climate, population, etc. of Verona and Mantua (where ROMEO AND JULIET takes place) with London and their hometown. Graphs, charts, and maps (MATH UNIT?) could be made to demonstrate the similarities and differences among the locales.

West Side Story

Clips of the Broadway musical can be shown and discussed.

Physical Education

Movement

Students can present interpretive dance, movement exercises or tumbling routines from the movie soundtrack of the play.

Combat Discussion

Discuss, show films or have resource person demonstrate sport of fencing and how it relates to the play.

Combat Experience

Use the clear and easy-to-follow techniques laid out in J.D. Martinez's COMBAT MIME (please see bibliography) to put together a stage fight.

Emoting with Movement

Have the students list on the board three different emotions found in the act you are studying. Ask them to move about the room (without speaking or making physical contact) as if they were experiencing one of those emotions. This can easily springboard into:

1) How does your body change when...

2) How does your breathing change when...

3) What has happened in your own lives to create such emotions...

4) How else can we communicate non-verbally, i.e., to say good-bye, I'm hungry, stop running, my leg hurts, etc.

Sports

Students research and work together on demonstrating a sporting activity during the century/place in study.

Mathematics

Graph and Compare

Decide on a criteria for the selection of "fighting" words and "loving" words spoken in ROMEO AND JULIET. Have the students count the number of each (spoken by each family and/or individual characters) and graph and compare results.

Scale Model of a Theatre

Compute an inches to feet ratio in order to build a replica of a Shakespearean theatre. After computing the ratio, students can draw or construct a scale model.

Science/Health

Computing Force

Students could hypothesize as many ways as possible that Romeo could have made his way to Juliet's balcony. Compute how much force would be needed to scale such a height given a selected weight for Romeo and a selected height for the balcony.

CPR

Use the death scene in ROMEO AND JULIET to motivate a discussion of cardio-vascular resuscitation. Have the students explain and demonstrate what they would have done to rescue Romeo and Juliet if they had happened upon the last scene.

Illegal Drugs

Juliet takes a drug to make it appear she has died. Students can present a report on different types of illegal drugs and all the reasons we should avoid them. A great follow-up would be to invite a guest speaker from a local agency to reinforce the dangers of illicit drugs.

Shakespeare Scavenger Hunt for Romeo and Juliet

(Please note gift from publisher at end of hunt.)

☞ Advise when hunt is to be finished.

☞ Number each item clearly.

☞ Printed material can be copied.

☞ Everything displayed in a box with your name on all four sides.

1. Picture of William Shakespeare.

2. Picture of the Globe Theatre.

3. Picture of someone in a sword fight.

4. Ticket stub or program from Shakespearean play.

5. Draw a picture of Romeo and Juliet at the balcony.

6. Write a one-paragraph description or draw how you feel Romeo or Juliet looked. (Only one of them.)

7. Draw a replica of Shakespeare's tombstone (bearing the famous inscription).

8. Completed copy of word puzzle on page 66.

9. In a small envelope place the amount of money a groundling paid to see a Shakespearean play.

10. Draw or trace the theatrical symbols of comedy and tragedy on an 8 1/2 x 11 sheet of paper.

11. Using the necessary maps (depending on your location) trace the route to the nearest Shakespeare festival.

12. A written list of all the Montagues (or Capulets) and all characters sympathetic toward the Montagues (or Capulets).

13. A list of the characters you felt sympathetic toward and one sentence explaining why.

14. Photograph of an individual with drugs and/or drug paraphernalia and a paragraph describing what that person's life might be like (in the worst scenario) a couple years from now.

15. The name of the character you most want to be like on a name tag that you design and a short paragraph describing why you want to be like that character.

16. Commit to memory at least seven lines of the play.

    (This activity can springboard into why you made that selection, how did you go about memorizing, what obstacles might stand in the way of actors trying to memorize lines, why is it important not to paraphrase when performing, etc.)

17. Design a bumper sticker that the young Montagues or young Capulets might put on the back of their cars if they lived today.

18. A copy of another play written by Shakespeare.

19. Display box with your name on all four sides with items numbered 1 - 19 inside.

20. Interview a teacher/professor AND a friend/family member that has read or seen a Shakespearean play. Find out what they liked best about Shakespeare.

(Each community's resources will be different. Some of these items may not be accessible. You might consider listing some items as 1) You can make on your own; 2) find in the community and/or 3) somewhere hidden in the classroom.)

Prizes

Each person to bring in all twenty items will be entered in a drawing for a lunch at a restaurant of his/her choice (or a prize you feel is more attractive).

Top three prizes — based on quality of work — will be judged by a panel of qualified judges.

1st prize...???

2nd prize ....???

3rd prize ....???

*   *   *   *

Gift From the Publisher!!!

Five Star Publications is happy to offer one signed copy of SHAKESPEARE FOR CHILDREN: THE STORY OF ROMEO AND JULIET (at no cost) as one of the Scavenger Hunt prizes. Please write Five Star with the student's name and a brief description of the student. Allow up to six weeks for delivery.

Romeo and Juliet

```
B A R D J F E C N A M O R E S C A L U S
G X A W U Y R O L A B R A M J Y A I B D
R O S I L T Y B A L T A Y Y E P R S Q N
O N A F I R R B O O X P C R P S O A U H
U E H E E A N T N V M I A M B I C N S A
N E T G T H O P E N E F O H M I K U A
D U L C M E T E R R P R G E W O S L S P
L Q A S H D J S P S P H Y M A N T U A O
I N B M I Y S S E A E L X O H T S M N T
N H U E S R S K H A T P A R U A C E N H
G O P R M Q A R F L E R W Y S G H L A E
F J H C S H C P V E R O N A B U O F O C
Y R T U S E W E I E F S O U A E O I R A
D A J T R A E P A H R E O D N X L V L R
E I U I P H M A L F G S Z I D O N E T Y
M R D O R C A P U L E T E E V F C S F O
O F I G H T E R S B H A M N E T B T O U
C S T E R F O A R O M E E C T S I A T E
Z O H R U O C Y L E N B L E C E S R H N
H P H I S T O R Y L L E W M O R C Z O A
```

How many names can you find?

BARD	PLAY	TRAGEDY	HAMNET
HUSBAND	WIFE	FIVE STAR	JUDITH
LISA	CASS	PRAY	SUSANNA
SHAKESPEARE	MONTAGUE	BALTHASAR	GROUNDLING
ROMEO	RAPIER	MERCUTIO	IAMBIC
JULIET	ESCALUS	ABRAM	METER
FRIAR JOHN	APOTHECARY	TYBALT	HISTORY
CAPULET	BENVOLIO	NURSE	ROMANCE
MANTUA	PETER	PARIS	CROMWELL
LOVERS	VERONA	SAMPSON	AUDIENCE
FIGHTERS	VIAL	HOPE	QUEEN
PROSE	VERSE	COMEDY	SCHOOL

(Five Star Publications permits reproduction of this page.)

Boredom

(Never in my class!)

Yes, as much as we hate to admit it, there have been situations where students became bored with the material. Fortunately, and in all honesty, those situations were extremely rare.

We are sure you have all sorts of tricks up your sleeve designed to prevent or solve this problem. Here are a few suggestions you can consider for **Shakespeare for Children.**

Bring in pieces of material and brooches/clips on the second or third day. Let the students doing the reading drape themselves in a "costume." They will come up with all sorts of costuming ideas and they'll love it. This is one reason we ask teachers to keep a record of who reads. We can't tell you how many disappointed children there were by the time the teacher started the fifth act and some students did not have an opportunity to read (in a costume!).

Have the students bring in news articles/books/theatre programs of Shakespearean plays/props they might use during the reading, etc. on a daily basis.

If you have an enthusiastic art person, s/he could create a background for the students to read in front of. One teacher drew an Elizabethan stage on a large piece of cardboard for the students to stand in front of.

Play Elizabethan music during the Capulets' masquerade party. Libraries are often helpful with period music or a school resource center could provide some.

Start your session with a related activity/warm-up that your students enjoy. This is especially helpful if your section starts immediately after lunch or P.E. You may decide the activity should be of the nature that helps center the youngsters, or settle them, rather than get them all hyper and rarin' to go.

Video-tape the readers and those following along. All sorts of possibilities with this one!

Seek out someone from a local theatre or university theatre department that might make a brief presentation on one aspect of the play or period, i.e., fight choreographer bringing in a rapier or dagger or a costumer bringing in costumes. Ask them what they might be able to offer to help stimulate the children's interest.

Arrange for an outing to see a Shakespearean play in your community or at a Shakespeare Festival. (Please see SHAKESPEAREAN FESTIVALS chapter.)

Performing the Play

It is very common for students to want to perform the play after studying it. This can be done with very little financial or technical assistance and you (the teacher) do not need any training or experience in directing. Things have gone pretty smoothly so far. They only get better!

Casting

We have found it is typical for students to actually do the casting amongst themselves. Whatever method you work with, it is important not to draft students into roles. We don't want them in uncomfortable situations - that would conveniently defeat what our work with this unit is all about. If the students are making the choices, you will want to gently guide them into selecting students with the ability to handle the more challenging roles.

There may well be the problem of more than one student wanting the same role. Have them solve that problem. Doublecasting will involve additional rehearsal time but may be the best option. It is perfectly acceptable for boys to play female roles and vice versa.

Rehearsing

It is advisable to work in small sections, rather than trying to go through the entire play each rehearsal. Take breaks when it appears concentration or focus is being lost. You may want to work with some of the warm-ups or other related activities from time-to-time.

Do not (we repeat, do not) feel the need for students to MEMORIZE their lines. It is fine for them to carry their scripts.

Give your actors plenty of feedback during rehearsals. If they are funny in a scene, it is OK to laugh. When they are finished, ALWAYS find something positive to say. Encourage them to determine what their character wants in a scene, how their character feels about the other characters in the scene and how they overcome the obstacles that prevent them from getting what they want.

Scenery/Props

An art teacher would probably love to help create a background or a scenic piece the entire play can take place in front of, and custodians might appreciate the opportunity to help build some swords made of dowel with funnel-like objects for handles (guards). Students and parents will also be great sources for putting scenery together. The important point is to keep it simple. Check out a video of a Shakespearean play and you will notice how neutral the scenery is. Props are more important because they will help the audience understand where the action takes place.

Costumes

A simple solution for costumes in ROMEO AND JULIET is to dress the Capulets in blue jeans and blue sweatshirts and the Montagues in blue jeans and red sweatshirts. Pieces of inexpensive material, brooches, pins, belts, tacky jewelry, hats, etc. put in the hands of a young, imaginative student will take care of the costuming. A parent or fellow-educator willing to help can serve as a coordinator.

The important point is not feeling the need to dress your students in period costumes. Such costumes are costly, time consuming and not at all what this unit is about. Your young actors can either dress in contemporary clothes, with no attempt to look like any other period, or they can dress in contemporary clothes and make a few adjustments that will suggest period.

Audience

We have discovered students are usually eager to perform the play before parents, friends, relatives and peers. Obviously, if you are performing in your classroom, you will need to limit the number invited. Video-taping your production may permit everyone an opportunity to see the play.

You will probably want to explain to the audience what has transpired over the past few weeks and that this is not intended to be a well-polished, professional production. The students (we hope) had a good experience studying the play and wanted an opportunity to share the story with you. Point out how much of the design, casting, etc. was accomplished by the students. We suggest video-taping the performance. Students might even want to design a program for the production.

If your audience is other (young) students, it would be highly recommended to conduct a session going over appropriate and inappropriate behavior when watching a live theatrical production. Ask them to help you list behavior in each category. Be sure to point out that it is certainly acceptable for them to laugh at something they find funny, to boo at something they find dastardly or to moan when something disappoints them, etc. We want them to be responsive, we just want to avoid distractions or any other inappropriate behavior.

Appreciation of
Students' Contributions

During the entire process you will want to praise the students for their contributions and ideas. The way this unit is outlined, it would be very difficult for a student to fail.

It is possible, however, for students to behave inappropriately. One way to deal with this is simply to begin the entire process by explaining this will be a time for creativity and you will welcome all their ideas and input. The only rule is that we are SINCERE in what we do. They must not confuse being creative as meaning a time that does not involve discipline or appropriate behavior.

At that point you will want to put the students in a hypothetical situation and demonstrate what sort of behavior would not be considered sincere. It may surprise you how effective peer pressure is once you get underway.

Once the entire unit is complete you might consider handing out some sort of award / certificate to each student. This is something you could make up or pick up at an educational supplier outlet. What you want is essentially something that recognizes their excellence in this Shakespeare unit. A photocopy of Shakespeare's portrait and quote from the play would be a nice touch. Computer graphics would certainly come in handy here.

Praise Suggestions

WONDERFUL   SUPER   OUTSTANDING   REMARKABLE

EXCELLENT IDEA   RIGHT ON TARGET   THAT'S INCREDIBLE

HOW INSIGHTFUL   GREAT DISCOVERY   FASCINATING IDEA

SPECTACULAR   MARVELOUS   GOOD FOR YOU   MAGNIFICENT

THAT'S CORRECT   HOW IMAGINATIVE   NICE WORK   VERY CLEVER

GREAT LISTENER   THANKS FOR YOUR CONTRIBUTION   ORIGINAL

VERY CREATIVE   THE TWO OF YOU WORK VERY WELL TOGETHER

NICE TO SEE YOU BEING ABLE TO WORK WITHOUT SUPERVISION

I APPRECIATE YOUR INPUT   EXCELLENT OBSERVATION   DYNAMITE

THAT'S BEAUTIFUL   HOW UNIQUE   VERY INVENTIVE

I'M PROUD OF YOU   THANKS FOR YOUR HELP   YOU'VE GOT IT

YOU'RE CATCHING ON   BRAVO   YOU FIGURED IT OUT

HOW CONSIDERATE   THAT WAS THOUGHTFUL   NEAT   WELL DONE

GREAT CONCENTRATION   THANKS FOR YOUR COOPERATION

WHAT A WONDERFUL ATTITUDE   THAT TOOK A LOT OF COURAGE

THANKS FOR SHARING THOSE IDEAS   THAT NEVER OCCURRED TO ME

RADICAL!

Promoting Your Class/School in the Local Press

If this unit is of special interest to your school or community, it will also be of special interest to the local paper, radio or television. It is extremely rare to find Shakespeare introduced below the fifth grade. Those schools introducing the classics for the first time, especially those of you working with this material as early as second or third grade, will probably find some interest in the media. Remember, while the language is condensed, you are working with the actual verse. That is not common, and it is not generally thought of as being accessible below fifth or sixth grade.

Administrators, school boards, and your colleagues will appreciate the public relations aspect; parents will enjoy seeing their child's photo in the paper; and the children, of course, will have scrapbook clippings they will cherish forever, but all of those reactions are only secondary to the sort of impact created by introducing your students to such quality literature in such a non-threatening manner.

You are a pioneer and unfortunately all too many of us in education are much too comfortable staying with the same lesson plans, lectures, exams and expectations. Preparing for this unit will take a fair amount of time and commitment but your willingness to explore this realm will reap far-reaching and far-lasting rewards.

Pronunciation of Names
For *Romeo and Juliet*

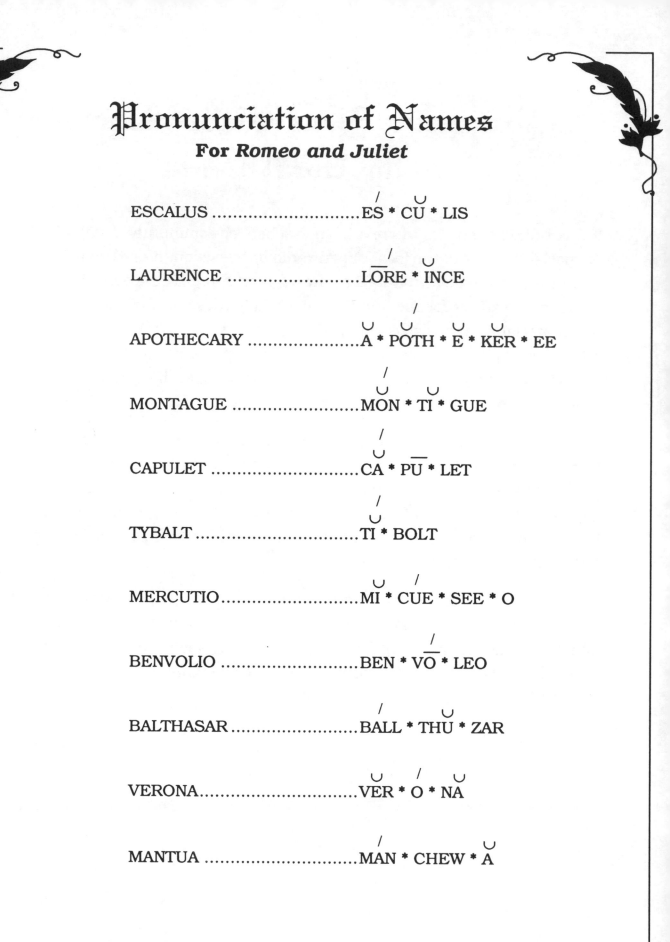

ESCALUS ....ES * CŬ * LIS

LAURENCE ....LŌRE * ĬNCE

APOTHECARY ....Ă * PŎTH * Ĕ * KĔR * EE

MONTAGUE ....MŎN * TĬ * GUE

CAPULET ....CĂ * PŪ * LET

TYBALT ....TĬ * BOLT

MERCUTIO........................MĬ * CUE * SEE * O

BENVOLIO ....BEN * VŌ * LEO

BALTHASAR......................BALL * THŬ * ZAR

VERONA............................VĔR * O * NĂ

MANTUA ....MAN * CHEW * Ă

Shakespeare Festivals in U.S. and Canada

Most festivals will gladly send you their season brochure with productions, dates, ticket prices and ordering information. Some of the festivals are even setup to accommodate tours and discussions with performers/designers.

ALABAMA SHAKESPEARE FESTIVAL
The State Theatre
P.O. Box 20350
Montgomery, AL 36120-0350

BERKELEY SHAKESPEARE FESTIVAL
P.O. Box 969
Berkeley, CA 94701

SHAKESPEARE THEATRE AT THE
FOLGER
301 E. Capitol St. S.E.
Washington, DC 20003

ILLINOIS SHAKESPEARE FESTIVAL
Illinois State Univ, CW 213B
Normal, IL 61761

CAMDEN SHAKESPEARE COMPANY
P.O. Box 786
Camden, ME 04843

SHAKESPEARE IN THE PARKS
Department of Theatre Arts
Montana State University
Bozeman, MT 59717

OLD GLOBE THEATRE
P.O. Box 2171
San Diego, CA 92112

COLORADO SHAKESPEARE FESTIVAL
University of CO at Boulder
Boulder, CO 80309

IDAHO SHAKESPEARE FESTIVAL
P.O. Box 9365
Boise, ID 83707

KENTUCKY SHAKESPEARE FESTIVAL
520 W. Magnolia
Louisville, KY 40208

BOSTON SHAKESPEARE COMPANY
52 St. Botolph St.
Boston, MA 02116

NEW JERSEY SHAKESPEARE FESTIVAL
Drew University
Route 24
Madison, NJ 07940

Shakespeare Festivals (continued)

NEW YORK SHAKESPEARE FESTIVAL
425 Lafayette St.
New York, NY 10003

GREAT LAKES THEATRE
FESTIVAL
1501 Euclid Ave.
Cleveland, OH 44115

OREGON SHAKESPEARE FESTIVAL
Box 158
Ashland, OR 97520

HOUSTON SHAKESPEARE FESTIVAL
Drama Dept, Univ of Houston
Houston, TX 77004

PARK CITY SHAKESPEARE FESTIVAL
2952 Arabian Drive
Park City, UT 84060

VIRGINIA SHAKESPEARE FESTIVAL
College of William and Mary
Williamsburg, VA 23185

CHARLOTTE SHAKESPEARE COMPANY
1236 E. Blvd.
Charlotte, NC 28203

NORTH CAROLINA SHAKESPEARE
FESTIVAL
P.O. Box 6066
High Point, NC 27260

THREE RIVERS SHAKESPEARE
FESTIVAL
B-39 Cathedral of Learning
University of Pittsburg
Pittsburg, PA 15260

UTAH SHAKESPEARE FESTIVAL
351 W. Center
Cedar City, UT 84720

CHAMPLAIN SHAKESPEARE FESTIVAL
Royall Tyler Theatre, U.V.M.
Burlington, VT 05405

STRATFORD SHAKESPEARE FESTIVAL
P.O. Box 520
Stratford, Ontario V5A 6V2

Chronology of Shakespeare's Plays

HENRY VI, PARTS 2 & 3	1590 - 1591
HENRY VI, PART 1	1591 - 1592
RICHARD III	1592 - 1593
COMEDY OF ERRORS	1592 - 1593
TITUS ANDRONICUS	1593 - 1594
TAMING OF THE SHREW	1593 - 1594
TWO GENTLEMEN OF VERONA	1594 - 1595
LOVE'S LABOUR'S LOST	1594 - 1595
ROMEO AND JULIET	1594 - 1595
RICHARD II	1595 - 1596
A MIDSUMMER NIGHT'S DREAM	1595 - 1596
KING JOHN	1596 - 1597
THE MERCHANT OF VENICE	1596 - 1597
HENRY IV, PARTS 1 & 2	1597 - 1598
MUCH ADO ABOUT NOTHING	1598 - 1599
HENRY V	1598 - 1599
JULIUS CAESAR	1599 - 1600
AS YOU LIKE IT	1599 - 1600

Chronology (continued)

TWELFTH NIGHT	1600 - 1601
HAMLET	1600 - 1601
THE MERRY WIVES OF WINDSOR	1600 - 1601
TROILUS AND CRESSIDA	1601 - 1602
ALL'S WELL THAT ENDS WELL	1602 - 1603
MEASURE FOR MEASURE	1604 - 1605
OTHELLO	1604 - 1605
KING LEAR	1605 - 1606
MACBETH	1605 - 1606
ANTONY AND CLEOPATRA	1606 - 1607
CORIOLANUS	1607 - 1608
TIMON OF ATHENS	1607 - 1608
PERICLES	1608 - 1609
CYMBELINE	1609 - 1610
A WINTER'S TALE	1610 - 1611
THE TEMPEST	1611 - 1612
HENRY VIII	1612 - 1613
TWO NOBLE KINSMEN	1612 - 1613

Bibliography

Abbot, E. A., A SHAKESPEARE GRAMMAR. Macmillan, 1966. (Compares Elizabethan grammar to modern grammar.)

Boagey, Eric, STARTING SHAKESPEARE. University Tutorial Press (UK), 1984. (Ideas and activities for introducing Shakespeare.)

Burgess, Anthony, SHAKESPEARE. Penguin, 1979. (Popular biography good for high school.)

Cottrell, June, CREATIVE DRAMA: GRADES 1-3. National Textbook Company, 1987. (Great ideas and activities.)

Cottrell, June, CREATIVE DRAMA: GRADES 4-6. National Textbook Company, 1987. (Great ideas and activities.)

Crosby, Nina, DON'T TEACH. LET ME LEARN. D.O.K. Publishers, 1981.

Engen, B. and Campbell, J., ELEMENTARY, MY DEAR SHAKESPEARE. Market Masters Books, Salt Lake City, UT, 1988.

Evans, G. Blakemore, et al., Eds., THE RIVERSIDE SHAKESPEARE. Houghton Mifflin Company, Boston, 1974. (A treasure! All of the plays, Shakespeare's life and times and general introduction.)

Fluegelman, Andrew, Ed., THE NEW GAMES BOOK. Doubleday/Dolphin, 1976. (Non-competitive games for all ages.)

Foster, Cass, THE SIXTY-MINUTE SHAKESPEARE: ROMEO AND JULIET. Five Star Publications, Scottsdale, AZ, 1990. (An acting edition complete with stage directions, definition of unfamiliar terms and simple suggestions for set and costume design.)

Haviland, V. (Ed.), CHILDREN AND LITERATURE: VIEWS AND REVIEWS. Scott, Foresman, Glenview, IL, 1973.

Hobbs, William, STAGE FIGHT. Theatre Arts Books, New York. (Fairly useful.)

Hodges, C. Walter, THE GLOBE RESTORED. 2nd edition, Oxford University Press, 1968.

Huck, C.S., Helpler, S., and Hickman, J., CHILDREN'S LITERATURE IN THE ELEMENTARY SCHOOL. Holt, Rinehart and Winston, New York, 1987.

Lane, Maggie, THE SHAKESPEARE QUIZ AND PUZZLE BOOK. Abson Books/ Burleigh Press, (UK), 1984. (Lots of fun material.)

Martinez, J.D., COMBAT MIME: A NON-VIOLENT APPROACH TO STAGE VIOLENCE. Nelson-Hall Publisher, Chicago, 1988. (Excellent and easy-to-follow guide to slaps, punches, falls, kicks, hair pulls, etc.)

Mills, E.B., ELEMENTARY ENGLISH: Children's Literature and Teaching Written Composition. 51, 971-973, 1974.

O'Brien, Peggy, TEACHING SHAKESPEARE: NEW APPROACHES FROM THE FOLGER LIBRARY. The Folger Shakespeare Library, Washington, D.C., 1986. (Video tape also available.)

Palffy-Alpur, Julius, SWORD AND MASQUE. F.A. Davies Company, Philadelphia, 1967. (Theatrical as well as competitive fencing.)

Pearson-Davis, Susan, WISH IN ONE HAND, SPIT IN THE OTHER: A COLLECTION OF PLAYS BY SUZAN ZEDER. Anchorage Press, New Orleans, 1990. (This has nothing to do with Shakespeare but excellent anthology of plays for young audiences.)

Sawyer, Ruth, THE WAY OF THE STORYTELLER. Viking Press, 1965. (Great tips for effective storytelling techniques.)

Schoenbaum, Samuel, SHAKESPEARE, THE GLOBE AND THE WORLD. Oxford University Press, 1979. (Great illustrations with discussion of Shakespeare and Elizabethan society.)

Schoenbaum, Samuel, WILLIAM SHAKESPEARE: A COMPACT DOCUMENTARY LIFE. Oxford University Press, 1977. (Plenty of useful information about the Bard.)

SHAKESPEARE: THE WRITING COMPANY. Culver City, CA (Excellent catalogue of books, videos, calendars, etc.)

Siks, Geraldine, CHILDREN'S LITERATURE FOR DRAMATIZATION. Harper and Row, 1961. (Another book that has nothing to do with Shakespeare but excellent source for those of you interested in dramatizing literature.)

Smith, F., WRITING AND THE WRITER. Holt, Rinehart and *Winston*, New York, 1982.

Spolin, Viola, IMPROVISATION FOR THE THEATER. Northwestern University Press, 1963. (Wonderful activities and ideas.)

Wilson, E. and Goldfarb, A., "LIVING THEATRE: AN INTRODUCTION TO THEATER HISTORY. McGraw-Hill, 1983. (From ancient Greeks to today.)

Teacher Evaluation

Five Star Publications and the authors are continuously seeking ways to increase the accessibility of Shakespeare in the classroom. What works and what doesn't work has largely been the result of feedback from individuals like yourself - individuals mentioned in the acknowledgments at the start of this book.

We invite you to respond to the effectiveness of this book and, if you are working with it, the overall effectiveness of the **Shakespeare for Children** series. Your comments, whether general or specific, will be read and considered by the authors. As the books are revised, we will gladly acknowledge those educators / administrators whose input is included. We also appreciate comments from students and parents.

Please direct your remarks to Five Star Publications. We thank you for your time and cooperation and wish you well in your introduction of Shakespeare to children.

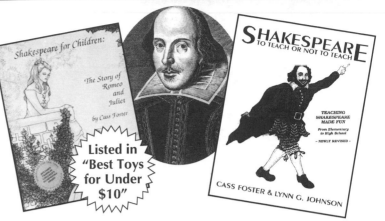